THE PENTAGRAM AS A MEDICAL SYMBOL

DR. J. SCHOUTEN

Director of the Municipal Museums of Gouda

THE PENTAGRAM

AS

A MEDICAL SYMBOL

AN ICONOLOGICAL STUDY

NIEUWKOOP   1968   B. DE GRAAF

8°. (II), 98 pages. With 41 illustrations. Supple boards.

f 18.— $ 5.— £ 2/2/— DM. 20.—

Medicine is rich in symbols, due largely to its close association with the weal and woe of humanity. A curious medical symbol which, as such, is now completely forgotten, notably the pentagram, the five-pointed star drawn in an unbroken line, is the subject of the present study. During the 16th century until into the 17th century, the pentagram was a well-known medical emblem; it is to be seen in armorial bearings, in the coat-of-arms of guilds, and in the frontispieces to medical and pharmaceutical works. Although the pentagram lost its significance as a medical symbol, it left its traces on the graphic arts and literature, traces which instigated research into the origin and meaning of this symbol.

The learned author devotes inter alia separate chapters to the pentagram in Antiquity, in the Middle Ages and in later times. The book is concluded by a Summary, a Bibliography, a List of illustrations and an Index.

Library of Congress Catalog Card Number 68-22990.

Orders can be sent to any bookseller or directly to the publisher

B. DE GRAAF
ZUIDEINDE 40 NIEUWKOOP / NETHERLANDS

THE PENTAGRAM
AS
A MEDICAL SYMBOL

by dr. j. schouten

DR. J. SCHOUTEN

Director of the Municipal Museums of Gouda

THE PENTAGRAM
AS
A MEDICAL SYMBOL

AN ICONOLOGICAL STUDY

DE GRAAF - 1968 - NIEUWKOOP

© 1968 - De Graaf - Nieuwkoop
Library of Congress Catalog Card number 68-22990
Translated from the Dutch by Miss M. E. Hollander, London

Printed in The Netherlands

To Prof. Dr. William S. Heckscher

CONTENTS

PREFACE

Tracing the origin and spread of a symbol is always a fascinating and often a worthwhile pursuit. Every symbol has a history of its own, gathering overtones during its passage through time, and it is exciting to follow its mutations as it takes its course. Originally, a symbol was merely an identifying sign, generally known and used for purely practical purposes; but it could be a secret sign recognisable only by initiates. Later in its history it took on the nature rather of an emblem; that is to say it became the visible image of something different, replacing an idea, or a representation of an idea, by another idea.

In our own times the word "symbol" has lost its ancient, profound meaning and has degenerated into little more than a badge, no longer based on, and expressing, a truth which takes the place of another truth.

Medicine is rich in symbols, due largely to its close association with the weal and woe of humanity. A curious medical symbol which, as such, is now completely forgotten, notably the pentagram, the five-pointed star drawn in an unbroken line, is the subject of the present study.

The pentagram, originally a charm against evil and, as such, also a talisman, passed through the stage of an identifying sign used by the Pythagoreans on its way to becoming a medical emblem or symbol.

Although the pentagram lost its significance as a medical symbol and became a forgotten chapter, it left its traces on the graphic arts and literature, traces which instigated research into the origin and meaning of this symbol.

The Author.

THE DEVICE OF THE GUILD
OF GOUDA SURGEONS

The visitor to "Het Catharina-Gasthu:s" Municipal Museum (formerly a hospital and called "Cathrijne-gasthuys") in the Dutch city of Gouda will come upon the Chamber of the Surgeons' Guild. On entering this chamber, he or she will be struck by the multiplicity of pentagrams — five-pointed stars with a radiating sun and human face at the centre —, the pentagrams themselves being crowned by two many-pointed stars (Ill. 1). These pentagrams will be seen on several beautifully worked cush:ons for the dignitaries of the surgeons' guild dated 1674 [1] (Ill. 2); also on the matching table cover showing the famous physicians Galen and Hippocrates bearing arms. On the far wall of the chamber there still hangs the instrument cupboard of 1699, with the pentagram and the date — the year in which the Gouda surgeons officially received permission to use this chamber as their guildhall [2] — cut into a scroll let into the bottom moulding. Until its dissolution in 1795, the guild held its meetings in this chamber. The centre of the beam across the great fireplace has been hollowed out to take an oval shield within a carved cartouche with a vegetal motif and "Anno 1710/11" [3] underneath, surrounding a pentagram carved in wood and polychromed (Ill. 3). Another item in the Guild's inventory which was retained is an 18th century cut-glass goblet on a silver foot, bearing a coat of arms with pentagram,

Ill. 2. TAPESTRIED CUSHION COVER WITH THE COAT-OF-
-ARMS OF THE GOUDA SURGEONS' GUILD, 1674.
*"HET CATHARINA-GASTHUIS" MUNICIPAL MUSEUM
OF GOUDA.*

topped with a crown, within a scroll, Louis XIV ornamenta-
tion running across below. On either side stand Cosmas and
Damian, one raising a urinal in traditional fashion, the other
an instrument bag [4] (Ill. 4). Just below the rim of the glass
the words "MEDICORUM ATQUE CHIRURGORUM
SALUS" are inscribed.[5] Lastly, the collection in "Het
Catharina-Gasthuis" also contains a 17th century brass seal,
the palm-wood handle of which once again bears the pentagram as the principal motif. This, too, comes from the
Guild of Gouda Surgeons.

10

Ill. 3.　DEVICE OF THE SURGEONS' GUILD OF GOUDA, 1710.
"*HET CATHARINA-GASTHUIS*" *MUNICIPAL MUSEUM*
OF GOUDA.

11

Ill. 4. GLASS GOBLET BELONGING TO THE SURGEONS'
GUILD OF GOUDA, SHOWING COAT-OF-ARMS WITH
COSMAS AND DAMIAN ON EITHER SIDE.
*"HET CATHARINA-GASTHUIS" MUNICIPAL MUSEUM
OF GOUDA.*

12

If we ask ourselves why the pentagram should be present in the Gouda surgeons' Guildhall and what this sign signifies, the answer is not far to seek. What we have here is undoubtedly the coat of arms of this guild, the pentagram being its principal element. As to the pentagram itself, it is surely a medical emblem or symbol and as such a distant echo of the Pythagorean emblem of health. The shining sun with its face placed in the centre of the five-pointed star suggests the unbroken tradition and continued influence of practical cabbalism. The two stars above the pentagram refer to the stars in the civic crest of the city of Gouda.[6] We cannot tell for certain when the Gouda Surgeons' Guild began to bear the arms with a pentagram. They applied to the magistrates and City Fathers for permission to found a "lawful and solemn guild" as far back as 1624, appending to their petition an "authentic copy of the public, signed and sealed letters patent" from the Emperor Charles V dated 6th February 1544, in which the Emperor confirmed the official recognition of their competence.[7] It was not until 16th December 1660, however, that the following entry occurred in the Records Office: — "Surgeons' guild charter granted".[8]

Although there is no documentary evidence one way or the other, it may be assumed that in 1660, the year in which the Gouda Surgeons' Guild was founded, the pentagram with the solar sign and Gouda stars was declared to be the official crest of the guild. As, after the Reformation, a purely Catholic patronage was no longer acceptable in the Northern Provinces, it is not surprising that the Gouda surgeons should have adopted an old pre-Christian symbol of health for the arms of their guild. To us in this day and age the pentagram may be a forgotten medical symbol, but in the 17th century it was not unknown in the world of learning.

13

[1]) Ontfangen bij mijn onderget. uyt handen van den Overman en Deckens van 't Serugijns Gijlde de somme van twee en vijftigh gulden thien stuyvers voor seven tappiste kussen bladen die op de winckel van Abraham Goossensom sijn gemaeckt actum den 8en Julij ao 1676 als gestelde Curateur van den boel van Abraham Goossensom Sr.   G. Boon   Bode

(Received by me the undersigned from the hands of the Master and Liverymen of the Surgeons' Guild the sum of fifty-two guilders ten stivers for seven tapestried cushion covers made in the shop of Abraham Goossensom this 8th day of July anno 1676 as appointed curator of the property of Abraham Goossensom Sr.)   G. Boon.   Messenger.
G. A. Surgeons' Guild No 17, appendices to cash books.

[2]) Den Overman en deeckens van het chirurgynsgilde wort geaccordeert een gildecamer in het Catharine gasthuijs van dese Stad, en worden de meesters en regenten van het voorsz. gasthuijs gelast het voorz. gilde daermede ten besten te accomodeeren.

(The Master and Liverymen of the Surgeons' Guild have been granted a guildhall in the Catharine Hospital of this City, and the governors and regents of the aforesaid hospital are commanded to accommodate the aforesaid guild to the best of their ability.)
Records Office, G.A., 110, fol. 38, 16th Nov., 1699.

[3]) ... Is bij overman en Deeckens geresolveert te late bekleede de schoorsteen (van onse Gilde kamer) met Lijstwerk en daer verder op te laten maken de wapens van den Regeerenden overman en Deeckens van 't Chirurgyns-gilde ...

(The Master and Liverymen decided to have the fire-place (in our guildhall) framed and, further, to surmount it with the coat-of-arms of the present Master and Liverymen of the Surgeons' Guild......)
G. A. Surgeons' Guild Resolutions Book 2, fol. 43, Oct. 1710.

[4]) The back of the glass shows the coat-of-arms of Dr. De Kedts with helmet, gem and mantling, and above it the words "HOCCE POCULUM DONO DEDIT D:D: DE KEDTS MED: DOCTOR". Dr. Daniel Dolegius de Kedts was Master of the Gouda Surgeons' Guild from 1723 to 1749.

[5]) An 18th century guild glass of the Surgeons' Guild at Rotterdam displays the arms of Rotterdam, likewise held by Cosmas and Damian, the representation deriving from the same design as that of the Gouda goblet.
Coll. "Het Catharina-Gasthuis" Mun. Museum, Gouda.

[6]) Although the official city-arms of Gouda has 6 stars, it also occurs with 2 stars. Cf. "Sigillum Opidi de Gouda ad causas 1408" and "Sigillum Opidi Goudensis 1490".

[7]) Cf. 6th vol. Corporation Records, G.A., 47, fol. 12, 10th Dec. 1601.
See J. Bik, "Vijf eeuwen medisch leven in een Hollandse stad", dissertation, Amsterdam 1955, 242. ("Five Centuries of Medical Life in a Dutch City".)

[8]) Records, G.A. 103, fol. 79, 16th Dec. 1660.

14

THE PYTHAGOREANS'
EMBLEM OF HEALTH

A curious passage by the Greek author Lucian [1]: *"Pro lapsu inter salutandum",* [2] will enlighten any reader who wonders how the pentagram could eventually also come to serve as a medical symbol in the West, notably in a little Old Dutch town like Gouda. Lucian relates how he was guilty of a breach of etiquette when greeting an acquaintance one morning, in that he saluted him with the words "Good health unto you" instead of "Joy into you". In extenuation, however, Lucian says that, although Pythagoras left no writings of his own behind, in so far as one could make out from Ocellus, Archytas and other disciples (ὁμιληταί), he gave precedence to good health (ὑγιαίνειν) over enjoyment (χαίρειν) or well-being (εὖ πράττειν). "All of his school, at all events, started their letters to each other, when they had anything important to write, with the exhortation to "be healthy" (ὑγιαίνειν παρεκελεύοντο), as this is best fitting to the soul and the body and, in a word, embraces all that is for man's good. And they called the threefold triangle, the pentagram, used as an identifying badge (σύμβολον) among their colleagues (ὁμόδοξοι), "health" (ὑγίεια). And, in a general way, they believed that good health is the root from which well-being and happiness spring (εὖ πράττειν καί χαίρειν) but that good health does not necessarily arise from well-being and happiness. There were some, moreover, who

15

Ill. 5. TESTIMONIAL ISSUED BY CORNELIS BLEULAND, SUR-
GEON IN GOUDA, IN FAVOUR OF ADRIANUS V.
BERGEN, 1ST SEPTEMBER 1785.
GOUDA MUNICIPAL RECORDS OFFICE.

also called the tetractys, which to them was the perfect number and by which they swore their most solemn oath, "the principle of health"; one of them was Philolaus.

In about 530 B.C., Pythagoras, b. at Samos in the 6th century B.C., d. at Metapontum *c.* 500 B.C., founded a religio-philosophical society at Croton, S. Italy, which spread to other cities and exercised considerable political influence. His followers, the Pythagoreans, can be divided into two groups, namely the akousmatikoi and the mathematicians. The former lived strictly in accordance with the dicta ascribed to Pythagoras himself (αὐτὸς ἔψα = he himself said it), practising asceticism and vowing secrecy as to the doctrine. The other group, the mathematicians, who did not accept the obligation of secrecy, adopted the scientific approach from Pythagorean premises to mathematics, music and astronomy.

The Pythagorean philosophy of life is closely bound up with the medical views held by the Pythagoreans. The main object of the guiding principles which Pythagoras impressed upon his pupils was to achieve a healthy balance between soul and body. The rule to avoid πολυτέλεια — excessive luxury — applied to the soul as well as to the body. As the Pythagoreans regarded illness as disordered harmony, they tried, by instituting a daily regimen of religious meditation, rhythmical body movements, gymnastic exercises and adherence to a diet, to lead a harmonious and healthy life.

The fundamental principles of present-day medical ethics are to be found in a passage called the "Hippocratic oath"; but it is not known for certain whether Hippocrates was responsible for the wording. The "oath" is probably older. Some authors are inclined to believe that it stems from the school of Pythagoras, which probably included some medical practitioners.[3] ὑγιαίνειν, good health, being so prominent a feature of the Pythagoreans' train of thought, the pentagram was an excellent symbol of health since, as a purely geometrical construction, it fitted in so well with their speculations as a symbol of balance and perfection.

Via Pythagoreanism the pentagram also acquired significance in Gnosticism. It is safe to assume, however, that, for astrological reasons, the five-pointed star (possibly the precursor of the geometrical pentagram) possessed some apotropaic value very much earlier in Babylon — that same Babylon where Pythagoras received his scientific schooling. This Babylonian five-pointed star represented a magic charm against evil influences. Later, especially in the Graeco-Hellenic world, it could be used as a shield against demons — the pathogens of those times — and also, therefore, stood for a symbol of happiness and health.

We shall presently see how, since the sixteenth century, the Signum Pythagoricum has come, more especially by way of Humanistic thought, to be accepted as a medical emblem in the West as well. First, however, it is fitting, I think, to take a more general look at the pentagram in Antiquity and at its area of distribution.

NOTES FOR "THE PYTHAGOREANS' EMBLEM OF HEALTH"

[1]) Lucian, Greek author (Samosata, Syria, *c.* 120 A.D.); initially a lawyer, orator and Sophist, later became a philosopher.

[2]) Ὑπὲρ τοῦ ἐν τῇ προσαγορεύσει πταίσματος

(Pro lapsu inter salutandum), *Luciani Samosatensis Opera,* Leipzig 1851, I, p. 330.

[3]) According to W. Leibbrand, the Pythagoreans were physicians in a certain sense, without exercising medical practice in a technical sense. Cf. W. Leibbrand, *Der Götliche Stab des Äskulab,* 3 Aufl. Salzburg 1939, 24, 28.

18

THE PENTAGRAM IN ANTIQUITY

The pentagram, a pentagon with added isosceles triangles drawn with one stroke of the pen, is a symbol whose origins are rooted in the culture of Mesopotamia. It is an established fact that it stems from Babylon, is the Sumerian sign UB, first found in the Uruk IV period, and dates from somewhere between 3000 and 2800 B.C.[1]

In course of time, the Uruk pentagram seems to have acquired a cosmic content, but this Uruk pentagram, the UB sign, is associated with the numeral four, not five. As a cosmic sign it may be connected with the planets Jupiter, Mercury, Mars and Saturn, corresponding to the four cosmic quarters and the four directions: forwards, backwards, to the left and to the right. As the fifth planet, Venus, "Queen of the Heavens" would, in that event, have been added to the other four.

It may well be that the Uruk pentagram itself was a geometrical figure. Ancient Babylon was acquainted with the regular pentagon, with which the dodecahedron was constructed. The structure of the pentagon presupposes knowledge of the geometrical pentagram.

In its pristine form, the pentagram probably had no apotropaic connotations, though it may be assumed to have acquired

19

these at a later period, possibly after the first millenium B.C. As a sign of the five planets mentioned, the pentagram had the potentialities of a talisman against the "evil eye" of many demons and spirits which, in the belief of the Ancients, were responsible for the diseases that assailed man and beast. From this it was but a step to its becoming a token of good fortune and health, among other things.

The pentagram, which is also called "pentalpha", because it consists of five times A, appeared in Palestine as well as Babylon. Many five-pointed stars are also found engraved in the tombs of Ancient Egypt, but they can scarcely be called pentagrams. In this case it may be a hieroglyph for a human being, or merely represents the stars. However that may be, the Egyptians did use the five-pointed star to represent the human body. It is certainly true that in Old-Egyptian art five-pointed stars stand for celestial bodies in representations of the firmament, which takes the form of a cow. Several guardian spirits support the body of the cow. In the centre is Shu, the god of the atmosphere. Along the belly of the cow, representing the firmament and showing many five-pointed stars, moves the heavenly barque of the sun god, on whose head rests the solar disc.

In representations of the goddess of heaven her body is likewise beset with five-pointed stars. Like an Egyptian Atlas, Shu lifts her aloft, while Geb, the god of the Earth, lies outstretched at her feet.

Both the pentagram and hexagram were familiar to the Jewish world from ancient times, but it is difficult, not to say impossible, to trace the origin of the two Jewish signs. It is nevertheless obvious that it was from Babylon that they spread, also to Palestine. It would, I think, be wrong to

Ill. 6.   THE PENTAGRAM ON A FRIEZE IN THE SYNAGOGUE
OF CAPERNAUM, 3RD CENTURY A.D.

assume that only the hexagram was of Jewish origin, whereas
the pentagram was not. In his *"Jewish Symbols in the Greco-
Roman Period"*, R. E. Goodenough states that both the pentagram and the hexagram were found on a frieze of a synagogue
excavated at Capernaum [2] (Ill. 6). This synagogue dates
from the beginning of the 3rd century A.D. In view of the
considerable intermingling of the two cultures in the Hel-
lenistic-Roman period, it is particularly difficult in this case
to discover whether symbolism of purely Semitic origin is
involved, or whether the influence of Hellenistic-Greek
thought has demonstrably come into play. The discovery of
Jewish earthenware jars with pentagrams and hexagrams im-
printed on their ears is more pertinent to the question as to
the origin and significance of the Jewish pentagram. According to David Diringer, who published these findings, [3] the

21

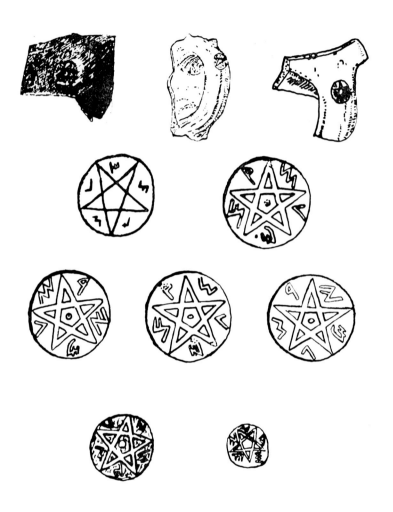

Ill. 7. PENTAGRAMS ON JEWISH JARS, PROBABLY 5TH CENTURY B.C.

22

jars came from the coastal regions of Palestine (Tel Zakariya and Gezer) and Jerusalem. The pentagrams are placed in a circle and bear an inscription of five characters between the points of the pentagram, neither the meaning nor the date of which is known. Diringer placed some of these jars in the 5th century B.C. and others in the 4th (Ill. 7).

In addition to the frieze in the synagogue of Capernaum, there is a fragment of a frieze bearing a five-pointed star, which was found in the synagogue of Chorazin,[4] referred to by Goodenough. He also mentions an early Hellenistic tomb at Marissa, in which graffiti with numerous pentagrams and hexagrams were found.[5] The tomb bears Greek inscriptions of around 200 B.C. The significance of the pentagrams and hexagrams in this grave is not understood. In the "Painted Tombs in the Necropolis of Marissa", Peters and Thiersch suggest that they are "Signs of greeting in secret and friendly intercourse,[6] which, therefore, would point to a Pythagorean influence." It is equally plausible, however, that they could be symbols of an apotropaic nature.

Ill. 8.   INSCRIPTION ON A TOMBSTONE IN TORTOSA, SPAIN, 4TH CENTURY A.D.

23

Lastly, I must mention an inscription on a Jewish tomb found in Tortosa, Spain (Valencia province), on which pentagrams likewise occur. It is an inscription in Hebrew, Latin and Greek [7] (Ill. 8), which must be placed somewhere in the 4th century A.D.

From the fact that the pentagram appears as a warrior's escutcheon on a drinking cup with red figurines it is evident that the pentagram was not unknown to the Greek world.[8] Here it is clearly a magic apotropaic or protective sign; and as such it also appears on a Grecian amphora, now in Munich (Ill. 9).

The pentagram is to be seen on many Greek coins; and it is surely due to them in large measure that the pentagram became so widespread as a symbol or magic apotropaic sign. The dates of the coins found run from the 5th century B.C. to a few centuries after the beginning of our era.

In an extensive study,[9] Professor C. J. de Vogel analyses Holger Thesleff's hypothesis [10] that there is a detectable continuity between the Pythagoreanism of the 4th century and that of the 1st century B.C. and that the Pythagorean Schools persisted in cultural isolation in Southern Italy, where, in the 3rd and 2nd centuries B.C., they produced school texts. Various coins on which the pentagram appears are among the evidence adduced in support of this alleged continuity. Here the pentagram would be the "Salus Pythagorae", the Pythagorean token of recognition and health, with a purely esoteric content. C. J. de Vogel points out, however, that even Croton, the bulwark of the Pythagorean School, did not possess any coins with a pentagram or geometrical figures at the time of the Pythagoreans.

24

Ill. 9.   AMPHORA WITH THE PENTAGRAM DEPICTED AS
ESCUTCHEON. MUNICH.

The pentagram appears as a symbol on coins deriving from Aesernia, Beneventum, Teanum Sidicinum, Velia; also on coins of the Bruttiers and the Mamertini, on specimens originating in Nuceria, Populonia, Cales, Cyrene, Syracuse, Rhodes and Rome. This pentagram, however, is likely to have been the old magical apotropaic sign deriving, as we have seen, from the Middle East, rather than one bearing the Pythagorean message. The same holds for a stater of Melos, which likewise displays a pentagram.

Ill. 10. STATER OF MELOS WITH PENTAGRAM.

Phoenician influence is known to have come to bear heavily on Melos coins, an influence, therefore, proceeding from the Middle East, the birthplace of the pentagram (Ill. 10).
The pentagrams on coins of the 4th century B.C. found in Thracian Chersonesus and in Macedonia should, I believe, likewise be regarded as representing the old magic sign. The idea that they are merely a decorative motif seems to me untenable.

Coins with pentagrams were in circulation throughout the Graeco-Roman world. They were passed as currency by the

26

soldiery, but also, and perhaps chiefly, by merchants, and were thus spread far and wide.

All the coins struck in Gaul displaying pentagrams and other devices are freely copied from Greek or Roman coins.[11] These, too, are unlikely to have been directly connected with Pythagoreanism and do not therefore stand for the "Salus Pythagorae". Either these Gallic or Celtic pentagrams are mere copies shorn of any content meaningful to these parts, or they have persisted in people's minds as a magic charm. This may well be so since, as we shall see, the pentagram survived as an apotropaic sign in Europe.

Though increasingly attenuated in content, the pentagram lived on in two ways from late Antiquity, through the Middle Ages and into the Renaissance. In one way it persisted in people's memory as the apotropaic shield against the power of a diversity of evil spirits, including the pathogenic demons. The other way is that of direct association with the "Salus Pythagorae", hence the Pythagorean symbol of both spiritual and physical health. The Pythagorean symbol, which is like the old Babylonian sign in appearance and inherently signifies health (ὑγίεια) as ideal harmony, without, however, possessing any esoteric magical power, was remembered mainly from literary sources and, therefore, by a comparatively small number of initiates, until the Humanists infused new life into it, though naturally as a mere echo of the old Salus Pythagorae. This renascence was undoubtedly supported and probably influenced by the concurrently existing and still remembered magical pentagram.[12]

NOTES FOR "THE PENTAGRAM IN ANTIQUITY"

[1]) Cf. A. Falkenstein, *Archaische Texte aus Uruk,* Leipzig, 1936, p. 118, under 453.

[2]) R. E. Goodenough, *Jewish Symbols in the Greco-Roman Period* (Bollinger Series), New York, 1953 (8 vol.); I, 187 for description; III, Figs. 473 and 474 for illustrations.

[3]) D. Diringer, *Le iscrizioni antico-ebraiche Palestinesi,* Firenze 1934, 130-132, pl. XVI, 3-12.

[4]) R. E. Goodenough, *Jewish Symbols,* I, 195.

[5]) R. E. Goodenough, *Jewish Symbols,* I, p. 68.

[6]) J. P. Peters and H. Thiersch, *Painted Tombs in the Necropolis of Marissa,* London, 1905, pl. IIIa; 19, 60.

[7]) *Revista de Filosofia del Instituo Luis Vives 15* (1956), 32-33.

[8]) *Museo Gregoriano,* prima ediz., parte seconda, tav. XC.

[9]) C. J. de Vogel, *Pythagoras and early Pythagoreanism* (series of philosophical texts and studies, Utrecht University) Assen 1966. Chapter III deals with the pentagram and Chapter X with the medical views of the Pythagoreans. Prof. de Vogel was kind enough to furnish me with many particulars about the pentagram and the Pythagoreans.

[10]) H. Thesleff, *An introduction to the Pythagorean writings of the Hellenistic Period* (Acta Acad. Aboensis, Hum. XXIV) Abo 1916.

[11]) J. Lelewel, *Type Gaulois ou Celtique,* Atlas, Bruxelles 1840, pl. X.

[12]) The same development is perceptible in the renascence of the rod-and-serpent of Asklepios compared to the Brass Serpent. Cf. J. Schouten, *The Rod and Serpent of Asklepios,* Amsterdam-London-New York 1967, p. 99 ff.

THE PENTAGRAM IN THE MIDDLE AGES

Jacob Grimm has pointed out that, in the sphere of German culture, the pentagram was known from ancient times as "Alpfusz", "Alpkreuz" and "Drudenfusz".[1] Owing to the similarity in sound, the word "Drudenfusz" is often erroneously associated with the Druids; erroneously, because "Drudenfusz" stands in relation to "Drude" (Alp), a tormentress who, in the folklore of Southern Germany and Austria, brings on nightmares,[2] against which the pentagram was supposed to possess apotropaic powers. The pentagram was also alleged to keep out other demoniacal beings, like witches and devils. It is in this sense that Goethe uses it in the first part of his Faust (verse 1935 ff.), where he says to Mephistopheles: —

"Das Pentagramma macht dir Pein?
Ei, sage mir, du Sohn der Hölle,
Wenn das dich bannt, wie kamst du denn herein?
Wie ward ein solcher Geist betrogen?".

Mephistopheles replies that the sign had not been drawn properly, there being a slight gap in the outside angle ("Der eine Winkel, der nach auszen zu, ist, wie du siehst, ein wenig offen").[3]

Ill. 11. STONE RELIEF WITH PENTAGRAM, 10TH/11TH CENTURY. IN THE 13TH
CENTURY THIS FRAGMENT AND OTHERS WERE USED TO LINE A FONT.
SPLIT, JUGOSLAVIA.

Ill. 12. WOODCUT FROM *PLUEMEN DER TUGENT,* AUGS-
BURG 1486. THE PENTAGRAM ON THE THRESHOLD
PREVENTS A WITCH FROM ENTERING THE BYRE.

As a talisman to ward off misfortune, the pentagram was
painted, or applied in relief, on household articles like cradles
and bedsteads (Ills. 11-16), against the walls of houses, on
cowshed doors, on castle gates (as, for instance, at Bentheim),
both inside churches and at the entrances to church buildings.
A fine example of the latter is the Norman (Romanesque)
porch of the church at Knauthain near Leipzig. After radical
rebuilding of the church in 1845/46, this porch was altered
to become the entrance to the vestry and there is a handsome
pentagram on the capital on the right-hand side of this
entrance,[4] which also goes to show that in the Middle Ages
the pentagram had also come to figure in Christian symbolism.[5]

There is another example in the Marktkirche of Hanover,

31

Ill. 13. ISRAHEL VAN MECKENEN, C. 1445—1503, NATIVITAS.
THE HEXAGRAM ON THE CRADLE IS IDENTICAL
HERE TO THE PENTAGRAM.

The robust tower of this church, which was begun in 1350, is topped by triangular gables, above which, in the original plan, a tall, octagonal pyramid was to have risen, but which now support a minute, four-sided spire. The gables are ornamented with an inset circle, in two of which (the north and south gables) there is a hexagram and in one (the east gable) a pentagram. Evidently here in Hanover, too, the hexagram and pentagram represent one and the same thing, the ancient apotropaic sign to ward off, and protect from, evil.

Ill. 14. PENTAGRAM (DRUDENFUSZ) ON THE INNER SIDE OF THE HEAD OF THE CRADLE. TWO ANGELS ARE DEPICTED HOLDING CHRIST'S MONOGRAM, IHS, ON THE OUTER SIDE OF THE FOOT, 1579.
Bayerisches Nationalmuseum, Munich.

33

Ill. 15.   VOTIVE TABLET FROM STADELECK, 1675. THERE IS
A PROTECTIVE PENTAGRAM ON THE OUTER SIDE
OF THE FOOT OF THE BEDSTEAD.
Bayerisches Nationalmuseum, Kriss collection, Munich.

Although the practice of adorning buildings, furniture, etc. began in the early Middle Ages, it obviously was not confined to mediaeval times, as witness the examples I have already given, viz., the cradle of 1579 (Ill. 14), the façade at Groenlo (Holland) dated 1621 (Ill. 16) and the votive tablet of 1675 (Ill. 15).

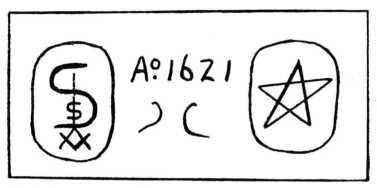

Ill. 16. HOUSE-SIGN WITH PENTAGRAM ON A FAÇADE AT GROENLO.

One also comes across the pentalpha on tombstones, as in the St. Janskerk, Gouda, for instance; also on fairly early fourteenth-century seals, reminiscent of a house-sign, but tinged, consciously or subconsciously, with memories of the apotropaic sign (Ill. 17).[6]

From Antiquity, the pentagram must have travelled as a talisman down through the Middle Ages. We have seen how coins provided an excellent means for spreading the visual image of the pentagram far and wide, though the Pythagorean symbol was only associated with it in a very minor degree. In the first half of the 1st century B.C., at the time of the Roman

Ill. 17. SEAL OF JAN WILLEM LAKENMANSZ., 1331.
Municipal Records, Gouda.

Republic, L. Papius [7] had denarii struck with pentagrams. As a renascence of Neo-Phythagoreanism was taking place just at this time in Rome, these coins may be connected in some way with the renewed interest in Pythagoreanism; but probably not. According to Sydenham,[8] the first-century B.C. coins struck by L. Papius and L. Roscius Fabatus are tokens of trade and handicraft, the representatives of which were associated in the Collegia opificum of Rome, the pentagram being the master-builders' badge.

36

Generally speaking, the pentagram was mainly an apotropaic sign in Antiquity and was well known as such, and as such it should be completely dissociated in our minds from the Salus Pythagorae.

In Early Christian times the pentagram does not occur at all, or, if so, very rarely.[9] This, in my view, substantiates the theory that the Early Christians abhorred the pentagram as a purely heathen sign. The same prejudice is to be seen in the hanging of garlands on sarcophagi. Popular though they were, they were scarcely ever hung on Christian sarcophagi, the only plausible explanation for which is that the Christians still regarded a garland as a non-Christian offering.

One of the uses to which the non-Christian world continued to put the pentagram was as a charm against evil applied to sarcophagi.[10]

Both in Antiquity and throughout the Middle Ages amulets, showing the pentagram among other signs, were in high favour. The fashion also gained a hold on the Christian world. St. Augustine complained that in his time (4th-5th century A.D.) old heathen incantations and invocations in Christian disguise had crept into medical writings and text-books and that magic practices were observed for medical purposes. St. Augustine had to contend with the old deities and more especially with those ill-defined powers, demons, which held the more ignorant in thrall. This dread of demons drove everyone, rich and poor, Christians and non-Christians alike, openly or clandestinely, to soothsayers, astrologers, quacks and the temple prophets. A great diversity of heathen amulets, even bearing the names of Christ, St. Michael and St. Gabriel as their device, were for sale.[11]

In permanent fear of poisoning (which, in the Middle Ages, was thought to include the plague and other infectious diseases), people sought desperately for antidotes against the mysterious evil. It is not surprising, therefore, that amulets of every shape and form should have been resorted to, even in the Middle Ages. Some of the most popular of these were "serpents' horns" and "serpents' tongues", called glossopetrae or glossites.[12)]

Until well into the Middle Ages and long after, demons, as a heritage from the past, were regarded as the principal causes of diseases. Consequently, in cases of illness a number of expedients with a religious tinge were resorted to in an attempt to exorcise the demons and, as has been said, ample use was made of mascots and amulets.

Well-known charms of this kind were the abraxas stones, sometimes called abrasax stones, also mentioned by Goodenough.[13)] These stones, originally Hellenistic gems and amulets often bearing the magic name of Abraxas, display an abundance of symbols, including the pentagram. Many of these Abraxas stones, which were alleged to derive from Syria, Egypt and Spain, were used as amulets and lucky stones in the Middle Ages.

Fossil sea-urchins were supposed to be particularly potent [14)] (Ill. 18). These have been found even in Neolithic graves, with a pentagram formed on the surface by Nature herself. The occurrence of the five-pointed star on the majority of fossil sea-urchins prompted some to lend Nature a helping hand if, by chance, the star on the surface of the fossil was not clearly enough delineated to be recognisable as a pentagram. The collection of Albert Ritter, who taught at the equivalent of the grammar school of Ilfeld at the beginning

38

Ill. 18. FOSSIL SEA-URCHIN WITH A PENTAGRAM ON THE
UPPER SURFACE.

of the 18th century, contains a touched-up sea-urchin of this kind.[15)]

An appraisal of the popularity enjoyed by the pentagram as a magic token in the Middle Ages should also take account of mediaeval symbolism, in which five as a number looms large. E.g., it is hallowed by the five books of Moses, the Pentateuch; by the five stones used by David as a weapon against Goliath; by the fivefold power in Jewish history, notably patriarchs, judges, kings, prophets and priests; by the five wise and foolish virgins; by the five talents in the Gospels; by the five hours spent by the labourers in the vineyard; by the five loaves in the miraculous feeding of the multitude; by the five Sacred Wounds of Christ; by the five mysteries of Christ, i.e., the Incarnation, Suffering, Resurrection, Ascension and Parousia in the latter day; by the five senses of man.

An echo of the holy number is also apparent in the liturgy, notably in the five crosses in the consecration of the Altar and the five crosses on the altar table, which are again the symbol of the five Wounds of Christ; the five grains of incense in the Easter candle; the five Psalms preparatory to Holy Mass; the five blessings above the Bread and Wine before the Consecration.

Below I quote some verses from a 14th century tale of chivalry called *Sir Gawain and the Green Knight*,[16)] considering them pertinent to the numerical symbolism in which the number five plays an important part, to which I referred above. The unknown author of this romance tells how the noble knight Sir Gawain carried the pentagram, depicted in pure gold, as the device on his shield. From the description the author gives of this emblem it appears that it was a figure drawn by overlapping lines, which is to say in a single stroke, called by the English "an endless knot".[17] The author dwells in some detail on the symbolism of the number five to explain why Sir Gawain used the pentagram as his escutcheon.

Sir Gawain and the Green Knight [18]
VI.
Then they showed him the shield with its shining gules,
With the Pentangle in pure gold depicted thereon.
He brandished it by the baldric, and about his neck
He slung it in a seemly way, and it suited him well.
And I intend to tell you, though I tarry therefore,
Why the Pentangle pertains especially to this prince.
It is a symbol which Solomon conceived once
To betoken true faith, which it is entitled to,
For it is a figure which has five points,
And each line overlaps and is bound with another;
And it is endless everywhere, and the English call it,
As I have heard, the Endless Knot.
Therefore it goes with Sir Gawain and his gleaming armour,
For, ever faithful in five things, each in fivefold manner,
Gawain was known as a good man and, like gold well refined,
He was devoid of all villainy, every virtue displaying
      In the field.
      Thus this Pentangle new
       He carried on coat and shield,
       As a man of troth most true
       And knightly name annealed.

VII.
First he was found faultless in his five wits.
Next, his five fingers never failed the knight,
And all his trust on earth was in the five wounds

Which came to Christ on the Cross, as the Cross tells.
And whenever the bold man was busy on the battlefield,
Through all other things he thought on this,
That his prowess all depended on the five pure Joys
That the holy Queen of Heaven had of her Child.
Accordingly the courteous knight had that queen's image
Etched on the inside of his armoured shield,
So that when he beheld her, his heart did not fail.
The fifth five I find the famous man practised
Were — Liberality and Lovingkindness leading the rest;
Then his Continence and Courtesy, which were never
corrupted;

And Piety, the surpassing virtue. These pure five
Were more firmly fixed in that fine man
Than on any other, and every multiple,
Each interlocking with another, had no end,
Being fixed to five points which never failed,
Never assembling on one side, nor sundering either,
With no end at any angle; nor can I find
Where the design started proceeded to its end.
Thus on his shining shield the shape of this knot
Was royally rendered in red gold on gules.
That is the pure Pentangle, so called by people wise
    In lore.

Ill. 19.   CABBALISTIC EMBLEM WITH PENTAGRAM, THE IN-
          SCRIPTION AGLA AND NAMES OF ANGELS.   ▶

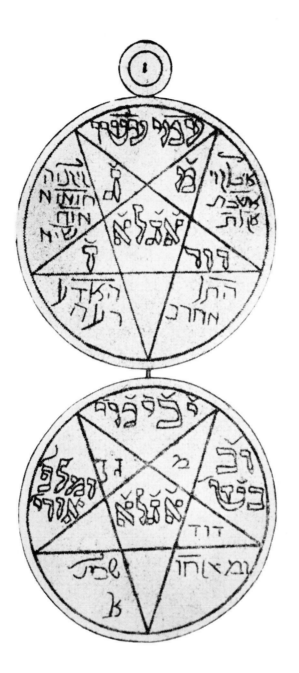

43

The pentagram also became an important emblem in cabbalism. In Jewish esoteric lore or mysticism, which, since the 12th century, has been the cabbala — i.e., "received doctrine" or "tradition" — one finds, among many other things, metaphysical speculations on the universe, the Creation and man's approach to God. The theories of the original cabbala were elaborated and worked over by later authors and thinkers. A distinction is made in the cabbala between theoretical (reflective) and practical cabbalism. The latter is indued with a magical character and makes ample use of amulets (some of which with pentagrams), incantations, the theory of numbers, and so forth. A fine specimen of a cabbalistic amulet with pentagram is to be found in "De amuletis" by J. Reichelt [19] (Ill. 19).

Perhaps practical cabbalism had something to do with the adoption of the pentagram as a masonic emblem by the Fraternity of Freemasons.

NOTES FOR "THE PENTAGRAM IN THE MIDDLE AGES"

[1] J. Grimm, *Deutsche Mythologie,* I, second edition, Göttingen, 1854, 419.

[2] H. Bächtold Stäubli, *Handwörterbuch des deutschen Aberglaubens* VIII, Berlin etc. 1936-7, col. 1173 ff.

[3] Also cf. Goethe *Maskenzühe,* 1818, 618 ff. "Mit Zirkeln und Fünfwinkelzeichen/Wollt er Unendliches erreichen".

[4] W. Stief, *Heidnische Sinnbilder an christlichen Kirchen,* Berlin 1938, 71 ff., Ill. 34, 38.

⁵) The same can be said of the rod-and-serpent of Asklepios, which, detached from the Greek god of healing, was associated with Cosmas and Damian in a mural at Dillingen. Cf. J. Schouten, *The Rod and Serpent of Asklepios. Symbol of Medicine,* Amsterdam-London-New York, 1967, 206.

⁶) Municipal Records, Gouda:
Jan Willem Lakenmansz., 1333.
Pieter Jan Lakenmansz., 1360.
Claes Jansz., 1364.
Jan Allaertsz., 1370.
Jacob Jansz., 1390.

⁷) A. Alföldi, *Schweizer Münzblätter* XII, Basle 1954, 27 ff.

⁸) E. A. Sydenham, "Symbols on the Denarii of L. Papius", in *Numismatic Chronicle* (1931), 5th series, part 11, 1 ff.

⁹) I am indebted to Prof. Dr. F. van der Meer for this information.

¹⁰) Roman sarcophagus. *Wallraf-Richartz Collection, Cologne Museum.*

¹¹) F. van der Meer, *Augustinus de Zielzorger,* I, Utrecht-Antwerp 1957, 66.

¹²) H. Pogatscher, "Von Schlangenhörnern und Schlangenzungen, vornehmlich im 14 Jahrhundert", *Römische Quartalschrift für christliche Altertumskunde und für Kirchengeschichte,* XII, Rome (1898), 169.

¹³) R. E. Goodenough, *Jewish Symbols in the Greco-Roman Period,* II, New York 1953.

¹⁴) O. Abel, *Vorzeitliche Tierreste im Deutschen Mythus, Brauchtum und Volksglauben,* Jena 1939, 227.

¹⁵) Fr. E. Brückmann, *Memorabilis Musei Ritteriani, Epistola Itineraria* XXXII, Wolfenbüttel 1734, 14, Tab. II, Fig. IV.

¹⁶) *Sir Gawain and the Green Knight,* Brian Stone, Penguin Classics 1959, vs. 642 - 690, p. 49 ff.

¹⁷) In a later form the pentagram was regarded as a magic knot, hence drawn in one continuous line. Apparently this idea did not predominate so much in Antiquity, when more emphasis was laid on the geometrical problem.

¹⁸) In "Appendix Six" the editor states that, in his notes on Sir Gawain, Sir Israel Gollancz writes: "According to the O.E.D. this is the only medieval example of the word, or any other compound of pente-, except Pentecost, Pentapolis. The next example of "pentangle" is in 1646". The pentagram was probably called by a different name in England, like Drudenfusz in Germany, but this name has not yet been traced.

¹⁹) J. Reichelt, *De amuletis,* Argentorati 1671, TAF. V, 1.

Ill. 20. DOCTOR ON HORSEBACK OUTSIDE AN INN WITH A HEXA-
GRAM AS ITS SIGN. *Kunstbeilage zum "Riedel-Archiv"*.

46

THE PENTAGRAM IN LATER TIMES

In later times the pentagram was sometimes shown on sign-boards, like brewery or inn signs [1]; currently, though now without any implied meaning, several industries use it as a registered trade-mark.[2] A curious example of inn signs is to be seen in a 19th century German print published under the title of *Kunstbeilage zum "Riedel-Archiv"*. The print depicts a doctor astride his horse surrounded by a crowd of onlookers while he takes a patient's pulse. A hexagram hanging from a beautiful wrought-iron bracket shows that all this is taking place outside the village inn. As in so many cases, here a hexagram is represented when actually a pentagram was intended [3] (Ill. 20).

A pentagram is often to be seen on flags and city coats-of-arms,[4] sometimes with an implied meaning, sometimes merely as an ornament. The five-pointed star on the flags of Morocco, Algeria, Turkey, Pakistan, Tunisia, Egypt and Indonesia is undoubtedly a Moslem symbol native to the Middle East and adopted from Jewry. The Arabs call it "Solomon's Seal". This Moslem symbol, in which the number five is the decisive factor, stands for several ideas, including God and Heaven. To this day protection and deprecation are mediated by the number five in the Middle East.[5]

The five-pointed star on the flag of the USSR, also appearing on those of the Peoples' Republics of China, Mongolia, Jugoslavia, North Korea, etc., symbolises the five continents. It stands in no relation to the old oriental sign, nor to the Salus Pythagorae.

The black five-pointed star in the centre of Ghana's flag and the yellow one in the Congo's must be taken as a symbol of happiness and hope, as a very remote echo of the ancient Babylonian protective sign, with which the Pythagorean symbol is likewise associated. No special symbolic meaning can be attached to the Star-spangled Banner, nor to the stars in the flags of Liberia, Chile, Cuba and Puerto Rica.

Strange to say, the Red Indians of North and South America apparently knew the pentagram as a charm against spirits in pre-Columbian times, and still do.[6] It is impossible at this stage to tell whether we are here confronted with a derivation or with a chance resemblance of a sign identical in shape and esoteric meaning to that prevalent in the Middle East. One might, indeed, venture even to think of an archetype (Ill. 21).

NOTES FOR "THE PENTAGRAM IN LATER TIMES"

[1] J. v. Lennep and J. ter Gouw, De uithangteekens (Signboards), Amsterdam 1868, 255.

[2] Cf. Texaco, now Caltex Oil Company, and Heineken.

[3] Fr. Röck, "Das Vorkommens des Pentagramms in der Alten und Neuen Welt", Globus 95 (1909), 7-9, note 1.

[4] Cf. the coats-of-arms of Maastricht, Nijmegen, Beuningen (Gelderland).

[5] Fr. C. Endres, Die Zahl in Mystik und Glauben der Kulturvölker, Leipzig 1935, 79-93.

[6] Fr. Röck, "Das Vorkommen des Pentagramms in der Alten und Neuen Welt", Globus 95 (1909), 7-9.

Ill. 21. MAGIC DEPRECATORY CHARM BEARING A PENTAGRAM, ▶
          FOUND IN BRAZIL.

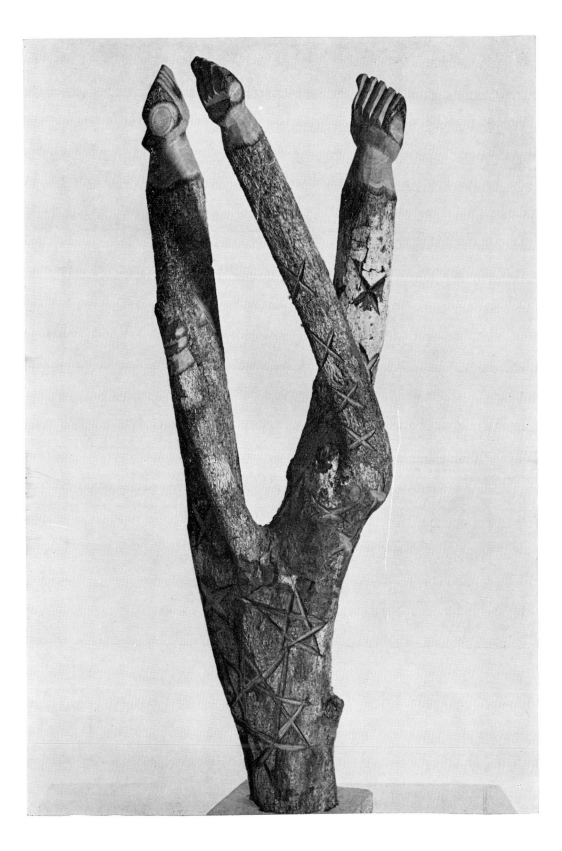

THE PENTAGRAM AS A MEDICAL SYMBOL

So far, we have been on the trail of the pentagram as an apotropaic emblem from early Antiquity to the present time, though in most cases shedding its esoteric content and ancient meaning in course of time and becoming a mere decorative element. I have already made it plain that the pentagram as a medical symbol, which was still recognised in the 17th and 18th centuries, should not be confused with the old apotropaic and protective charm.

The medical symbol undoubtedly goes back to the Signum Pythagoricum, valued for its pure geometrical construction and becoming the symbol of mental and physical health without any magical implications at all. As such it became the token of Pythagorean philosophy. It is difficult to deny, however, that the Pythagoreans' choice of the pentagram as their symbol may well have been influenced to some extent by the co-existent and much earlier apotropaic sign.

As from the Renaissance, the pentagram as a medical symbol has its roots in the sphere of iatromathesis — i.e., astrological medicine — and is, therefore, but a faint echo of the purely Pythagorean emblem. The signs of the zodiac played a dominant part in this "art". The renascence of the Pythagorean health token was strongly influenced by practical cabbalism,

51

a prominent feature of which was the practice of astrology. Admittedly, the starting point from literary sources was the emblem of the Pythagoreans, for whom the perfect harmony of the geometrical construction of the pentagram became, *ipso facto,* the symbol of health; but at the same time it became loaded with the underlying meaning of an older and, more especially, astrologically biased content.

Paracelsus [1] pointed out that, being a sign of the Microcosm, the pentagram played a very important part in the practice of magic.[2]

To Agrippa von Nettesheim [3] the pentagram is the expression and embodiment of the harmony that exists between the Microcosm and the Macrocosm. He says that man, being the most beautiful and accomplished work of God, made in His image and a world in miniature, has a body more perfectly and harmoniously constructed than that of the rest of Creation. It contains all the numbers, dimensions, weights, movements, elements; in a word, everything that makes a finished work complete; and in it, as in the loftiest masterpieces, attains to a degree of perfection not possessed by other complex bodies. For example, the dimensions of human limbs stand in definite relations to each other and harmonise with the members of the world and the dimensions of the Archetype so exactly that there is no member of the human body that does not correspond to a sign in the heavens, a star, an intelligence, a divine name in God's prototypes... Thus Agrippa von Nettesheim, who, in his *De occulta Philosophia* (1531),[3] describes the pentagram as an emblem revealing the simplest, pure synthesis of the human figure. He places the latter in the pentalpha circumscribed by two circles, in the following manner: The head is in the point of contact of pentagram and circle, the arms and legs stretched, the fingers and toes

52

likewise in the points of contact. The signs of the Zodiac, Mars, Venus, Mercury, Saturn and Jupiter [4] (Ill. 22), appear at the vertices of the pentagram.

Agrippa von Nettesheim's second example is a small pentagram in four concentric circles having signs of the planets as the circumscription. A note by the author states that this is the ὑγίεια or sign of health used as a badge by Antiochus surnamed Soter, to which he owed his conquest.[5] Hence in this case it is once more a protective and apotropaic device, the mention of ὑγίεια pointing to its Pythagorean origin.

The pentagram also appears in the *Hieroglyphica* of Pierius Valerianus (1477-1558), the first great manual of symbols, reprinted many times. Valerianus illustrates a pentagram placed in a circle, stating that this is the sacred sign of Lucianus, hence the Pythagorean symbol of health.[6] He depicts another pentagram with ΥΓΕΙΑ as its circumscription and states, as did Von Nettesheim, that this is the health sign of Antiochus Soter. Antiochus, a member of the Seleucid dynasty famed for his conquest of the Galatians, had a pentagram emblazoned on his warriors' armour before the battle. Afterwards he also had the pentagram inscribed on his coins.[7]

Valerianus connects a third pentagram with the five wounds of Christ. The figure of Christ is partly covered by the pentagram, the wounds being touched by the five points of the symbol.[8]

It is evident that Valerianus, the Humanist, knows the "Salus Pythagorae" from his quotation of Lucianus, but also that he associates the old apotropaic content with the pentagram and finally raises it to the status of a Christian symbol. He gives

53

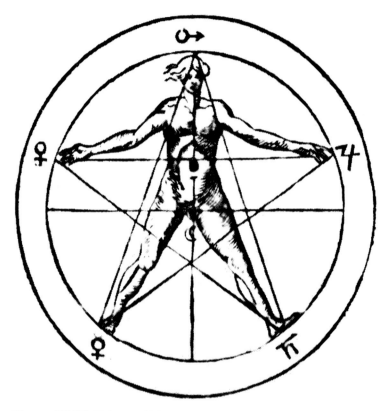

Ill. 22. PENTAGRAM WITH HUMAN FIGURE IN: AGRIPPA AB NET-
TESHEIM, *DE OCCULTA PHILOSOPHIA,* FIRST EDITION,
ANTWERP, ETC. 1531.

no hint, however, of regarding it as a true medical emblem or symbol.[9]

I referred earlier to the association of the pentagram with ancient astrology and to the habit of placing the signs of the five planets between the points of the pentalpha. The pentagram was also regarded as the perfect and simplest synthesis of the human figure, which was sometimes depicted in this symbol, the underlying idea undoubtedly being that the macrocosm of the spheres was reflected in the human microcosm. This at the same time established the principle of d'viding the human body to correspond to the 12 points of heaven and the 12 signs of the zodiac.

On what was called a "blood-letting mannikin", derived in its turn from the zodiacal mannikin, the twelve parts of the body were connected with the twelve signs of the zodiac controlling these parts of the body. The sign of the Ram was supposed to affect the head, that of the Bull the throat and neck, the Twins were responsible for the shoulders and arms, the Crab controlled the chest, the royal Lion held sway over the heart, the Virgin governed the belly, the Balance the loins and the Scorpion the genitals. The thighs are the Archer's province, the knees the Goat's, the shin-bones the Waterbearer's and, lastly, the feet the Fishes'.

It being assumed that a planet could strengthen or weaken the sphere of influence of a certain constellation, it was necessary to know the exact position of the planets with respect to the zodiac before undertaking a venesection; moreover, the choice of the proper vein for the blood-letting was determined by knowledge of that exact position.

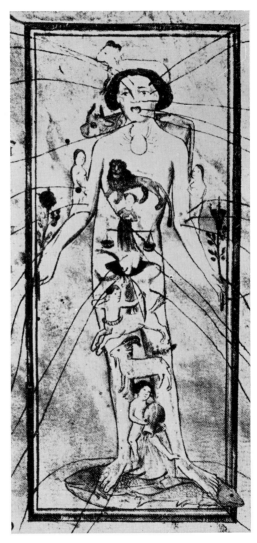

Ill. 23. BLOODLETTING MANNIKIN,
BEGINNING OF 15TH CENTURY.
Bibliothèque Nationale, Paris.

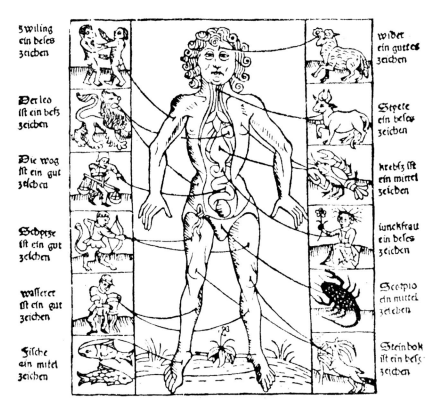

Ill. 24. BLOODLETTING MANNIKIN, BLOODLETTING ALMANAC,
15TH CENTURY.

Doctors of medicine were expected to be thoroughly ground-
ed in astrology; the demands made on surgeons in this respect
were less exacting. As, however, it was precisely surgeons
who had to do the blood-letting, they used the blood-letting
mannikin which one comes across again and again from the
Middle Ages right down to the 19th century, both in medical
works and as popular illustrations on blood-letting almanacs
and the like. By means of the signs of the zodiac, the mannikin indicates the most propitious part of the body for
successful blood-letting at any given moment (Ills. 23, 24).[10]
It is within this context that the renascence of the pentagram
as an emblem of health takes place; hence certainly not as a
mere repetition of the Pythagorean symbol, of which it is
only a reflection with, perhaps, connotations of the ancient
and still existing apotropaic sign and strongly influenced by
iatromathesis.

It is clear from early books on emblems that Antiochus
Soter's emblem of health, i.e., the Salus Pythagorae used by
Soter as his armorial bearings in his battle against the
Galatians, became a sign of protection. It is also evident in
Le imagini de i dei gli antichi by Vincenzo Cartari (1571).
Cartari includes the pentagram, with a drawing of the symbol,
in his list of signs and emblems. He calls the pentagram a
Segno della Salute in forma di Pentagone in contradistinction
to the rod-and-serpent of Asklepios, which he calls Segno di
sanità.[11] Cartari furthermore states that this sign also
appears on one of Antiochus' coins, repeating the well-known
story of the battle against the Galatians. In his drawing of the
pentagram, Cartari surrounds it with the words Salus and
ΥΓΕΙΑ, with the letters of the two words alternating (Ill. 25).
The printer's device adopted by Johannes Heyl was undoubtedly inspired by Antiochus Soter's pentagram. On 28th
August 1517 Johannes Heyl was entered in the register of

58

ma spelonca, e tanto imbalordito, & attonito che non si ricorda
ua più di se stesso, ne di altri. Ma gli Sacerdoti, che erano qui-
ui per questo, lo rimetteuano in un seggio, che si dimandaua la
Sede della memoria, e gli risoueniua allhora tutto quello che ha-
ueua uisto, et udito, e raccontaualo à que' Sacerdoti, che ne tene-
uano conto. Dapoi à poco a poco andaua ritornando in se: e si pò
credere che ui hauesse buona stretta, perche pochi furono quelli,
che ridessero mai più poscia che erano stati nell' antro di Trofo-
nio. Racconta molte altre cose Pausania, che si faceuano per an-
dare à questo Oracolo, e dice di esserui stato egli stesso : ma io ne
ho detto così breuemēte per mostrare solo chi fosse costui, cui era
no non meno che ad Esculapio consecrati i serpenti. Cicerone par
lando della natura de i Dei dice che ui furono molti Mercurij, e
che di questi uno staua sotterra, et era il medesimo che Trofonio.
Furono i serpenti appresso de gli antichi segno di sanità, perche
come il serpēte posta giù la uecchia spoglia si rinuoua, così paiono
gli huomini risanādosi essere rinouati. E perciò fu da questi fatta
la imagine della Salute in questo modo. Staua una donna à sede
re in alto seggio con una tazza in mano, & haueua un' altare ap
presso, sopra delquale era un serpēte tutto in se riuolto, se non che
pure alzaua il capo. Fassi anchora il segno della Salute in forma
di Pentagono, come si uede nelle medaglie antiche di Antioco,

del quale si legge che facendo guerra già
contra i Galati, e trouandosi à mal parti
to, uide, ò che per fare animo à soldati fin
se di hauere uisto Alessādro Magno, che
gli porgeua questo segno, dicendogli, che
lo douesse dare à Soldati, e fare che lo por

L   2   *tassero*

Ill. 25.   THE PENTAGRAM AS EMBLEM OF HEALTH IN VINCENZO
CARTARI'S *LE IMAGINI DE I DEI DE GLI ANTICHI*,.......,
VENICE 1571, p. 91.

the medical faculty at Cologne University. From 1519 onwards he printed and published books. His medical knowledge is evident from a foreword he wrote for a *Dioscorides* published by him, as is his linguistic knowledge from an edition of the *Psalms* in several languages. Heyl hellenised his German name to Soter (Antiochus), at the same time adopting Soter's emblem, the pentagram, for his device, thereby very ingeniously symbolising his own name and at the same time emphasizing his medical activities by means of this emblem of health for his device or family coat of arms. (Heyl is the old spelling of the German word Heil). It is not clear what the signs in the corners of the pentagram are meant to convey. There can be no question of a mutilation of the characters ὑγίεια , as Heyl was well versed in Greek. They are more probably corrupted hieroglyphic signs of the zodiac. In 1528 I. Soter of Cologne published *De asse et partibus eius,* in which the printer's device appears as a pentagram held by two cherubs (Ill. 26). His son Melchior Soter, established at Dortmund as a printer and publisher, likewise bore the pentagram with the same puzzling signs. Melchior's device bears the circumscription Symbolum Sanitatis [12] (Ill. 27).

Sanitas personified as a woman appears in a beautiful copper engraving by Dirk Volkertsz. Coornhert (1519-1590), one of a series of various allegorical presentations.[13] On a large oval dish she carries the pentagram — drawn in one stroke, be it understood — and a urinal. Since the Middle Ages the urinal, more so than the rod-and-serpent of Asklepios or the pentagram, had been the supreme badge of medical practice.[14] Over and above this, Sanitas carries a bird with a stone in its beak on her head; this is obviously intended to represent a crane carrying a stone, a symbol of vigilance and, therefore, a medical symbol.[15] The word *Sanitas* is inscribed under the figure of the woman (Ill. 28).

60

צִיר אֱמוּנִים לְמַרְפֵּא

Ill. 26. I. SOTER'S PRINTER'S DEVICE IN IO GROLIERIO, *DE ASSE ET PARTIBUS,* COLOGNE 1528.

Ill. 27. MELCHIOR SOTER'S PRINTER'S DEVICE IN TARQUINIUS
SCHNELLENBERG, *WETTERBUCHLIN*, DORTMUND 1549.

62

Ill. 28. DIRK VOLKERTSZ. COORNHERT, 1519—1590, *SANITAS*. (DE-TAIL) *PRINT ROOM "HET CATHARINA-GASTHUIS" MUNI-CIPAL MUSEUM, GOUDA.*

The pentagram in this engraving is without doubt a medical symbol. As Coornhert later went to Gouda, where he died in 1590 and was buried in St. John's Church, the Gouda surgeons may quite possibly have known this engraving with the pentagram as a symbol of health.

An engraving by Th. Galle (1571-1633) depicts Sanitas in the guise of a woman, patently inspired by *Medicina* and *Sanità* as they appear in Cesare Ripa's *Iconologia*.[16] In our engraving a woman is holding a sturdy rod-and-serpent in her left hand, and a pentagram, looking rather like a starfish, in her right hand. A urinal and an ointment jar lie at the feet of Sanitas and the name *Sanitas* is inscribed above the figure. Together with the rod-and-serpent, the urinal and the ointment jar, the pentagram is here undoubtedly intended as a medical symbol (Ill. 29). The frontispiece of the *Ars Magnetica* by Athanasius Kircher (1601-1680), published in 1654, includes the pentagram among the many other symbols representing the spiritual and worldly powers (Ill. 30). In addition to the customary ΥΓΕΙΑ spaced out between the five points, this pentagram has the word *Medicina* as its circumscription. Kircher intended this pentagram to be a medical symbol.

As the Gouda Library contained many works of Kircher's from early times, it is not unreasonable to suppose that this frontispiece, too, may have played some part in the Gouda surgeons' choice of their Guild's coat of arms in 1660. Admittedly, however, the *Hieroglyphica of Valerianus* referred to above was probably among the early collection in this library; so the Gouda surgeons had ample sources of information.

In his *Schat der Gesontheyt* (approx. Treasure-house of

Ill. 29. TH. GALLE, 1571—1633, *SANITAS.*

Health) of 1672, Joh. van Beverwyck includes a poem by
Jacob Cats bearing the title "Van de Gesondtheyt, en haere
Weerdigheyt" (On Health and its Value), a hymn of praise
to Hygieia. To this Van Beverwyck adds his own observations
on health and refers to the emblem of Pythagoras and Antiochus. These observations are illustrated by a rather me-
diocre copper engraving in which the goddess Hygieia is seen
sitting as a stylite on a very tall socle shaped like an antique
round altar. The goddess is surrounded by people with palm
twigs and raised globlets to "... give her the toast of good
health... which we therefore also call Santé".

Ill. 30.   ATHANASIUS KIRCHER, *Ars Magnetica, ROME 1654,*
FRONTISPIECE (DETAIL).

Ill. 31. HYGIEIA WITH HEXAGRAM (FOR PENTAGRAM), ILLUSTRATION IN *Schat der Gesontheyt* BY JOH. VAN BEVERWIJCK, AMSTERDAM 1672.

A horn of plenty and, under it, the hexagram as the emblem of health decorate the front of the socle. This is plainly another instance of the mistaken use of the six-pointed star instead of the pentagram. Van Beverwyck's description of the sanitas symbol is rather peculiar: "… three interwoven circles, representing the Greek characters of health" (Ill. 31).

The frontispiece of *De Purgentibus Exercitatio* by Joh. Nicolaus Pechlin, Leyden and Amsterdam 1672, shows Asklepios as a teacher, pointing with his left hand to a large anatomical chart and stirring with his rod in the other hand a number of medicinal herbs on a table beside the bed on which a

67

patient is lying. The Aesculapian serpent is coiled on the sickbed. Asklepios' daughter Hygieia, a pentagram on her head, is standing beside him. The nature of this emblem of health is further underlined by the circumscription SALUS and ὑγίεια, the letters of the two words alternating. This pentagram is a replica of that published by Vincenzo Cartari in 1571 [18] (Ill. 32).

Hygieia, with the pentagram and SALUS circumscription on her head, appears yet again in the very elaborate and highly remarkable frontispiece of *Metamorphosis Aesculapii et Apollinis Pancreatici* (1693) by *Jani Leoniceni Veronensis* (pseudonym for Joh. Nicolaus Pechlin). In this work, according to Mollerus (*Cimbria Literata,* 1744), he "attacks his own teachers Sylvius and Reinier de Graaf with biting derision". In the print, engraved by H. Friedlein, Hygieia is sitting in a scholar's study with flowers and plants in her hand and lap. The character of the room is accentuated by a large bookcase with books and numbers of folios in the foreground. The learned man himself is sitting at his table explaining something while pointing to a naked man standing in front of him. A statue of Mercury with his caduceus is seen in a niche in the background (Ill. 33).

The same frontispiece appears in the *Observatio - Numphysico Medicarum* by Johannes Nicolaus Pechlin, published in Hamburg in 1691.

The frontispiece of the book *Ontleeding des menschelijken lichaems* (Anatomy of the Human Body), written by Gerardus Blasius and published at Amsterdam in 1675, shows Asklepios, holding his rod-and-serpent and with the pentagram behind his head by way of a halo, watching an anatomical dissection, while Apollo overlooks the whole scene from above (Ill. 34).

68

I:N:PECHLINI
DE
PURGANTIBUS
EXERCITATIO.

Lug:Bat: et Amstell. apud GAESBERIOS 1672.

Ill. 32. JOH. NICOLAUS PECHLIN, *DE PURGANTIBUS
EXERCITATIO,* LEYDEN AND AMSTERDAM, 1672.

Ill. 33. *JANI LEONICENI VERONENSIS* (JOH. NICOLAUS PECHLIN)
METAMORPHOSIS AESCULAPII ET APOLLINIS PANCREATICI,
1673.

70

Ill. 34. GERARDUS BLASIUS, *ONTLEEDING DES MEN-SCHELIJKEN LICHAEMS* (ANATOMY OF THE HUMAN BODY), AMSTERDAM 1675, FRONTISPIECE.

71

The pentagram, intended as a medical symbol, also appears in the frontispiece (engraved by A. Schoonebeek) of Johan Conrad Peyer's *Parerga anatomica et medica*, Amsterdam, 1682.[19] The engraving depicts the anatomical study of both the human and animal body; and as usual Apollo, the supreme god of medicine, surveys the scene from his throne above the clouds. Salus, symbolising the art of medicine, is present at the dissection, wearing the pentagram with its SALUS circumscription on her head (Ill. 35).

The title-page of the *Parerga Anatomica et Medica* has a vignette (woodcut) showing Asklepios seated, raising his rod-and-serpent aloft. The pentagram with SALUS stands on a truncated obelisk behind the god of healing (Ill. 36).

Romein de Hooghe engraved the frontispiece for the first edition of the Pharmacopoea Harlemensis (1693).[20] De Hooghe himself wrote a poem, *Explanatio Tabulae Dedicatoriae Coll. Med. Pharmaceutico Data a Romana de Hooghe*, explaining the ideas incorporated in the frontispiece. In the latter Hygieia, the central figure, stands in a dispensary. She is wearing a gown with many eyes depicted on it to represent vigilance, because the goddess is preparing a theriac.[21] She is treading on a snake and in her left hand carries a chain attached to three figures. Hygieia is crowned by the pentagram as a medico-pharmaceutical symbol surrounded by the word *Salus*. De Hooghe forgot to engrave the word *Harlemensis* on his frontispiece, an omission that was not corrected until 1741 [22] (Ill. 37). A variant of De Hooghe's engraving is to be seen in the frontispiece of the *Haarlemmer Apotheek*, an illegal translation and edition published by Abraham Bogaert at Amsterdam in 1693. In this engraving Hygieia carries the Salus symbol on her head.

72

Ill. 35. JOHAN CONRAD PEYER, *PARERGA ANATOMICA,*
AMSTERDAM 1682, FRONTISPIECE
BY ADRIAEN SCHOONEBEEK.

73

JOH. CONR. PEYERI
PARERGA
ANATOMICA
ET
MEDICA,
SEPTEM

Ratione ac experientia parentibus
concepta & edita.

ONSULTORIBUS

AMSTELÆDAMI,
Apud HENRICUM WETSTENIUM.

CIƆ IƆC LXXXII.

Ill. 36.   JOHN. CONR. PEYER, *PARERGO ANATOMICA ET MEDICA,*
AMSTERDAM 1682. TITLE-PAGE, WOODCUT.

Ill. 37. *PHARMACOPOEA HARLEMENSIS*, 1693. FRON-
TISPIECE BY ROMEIN DE HOOGHE.

A hexagram appears under the scroll bearing the name of the medicine on several 18th century German flagons and glass jars. Once again, the five-pointed and six-pointed stars are mistakenly interchanged; for the hexagram on this pharmaceutical glasswork is the old Salus sign which became a medical symbol, and nothing but that. Above the scroll is a sun with a face throwing out its beams similar to that on the pentagram of the Gouda Surgeons' Guild (Ill. 38).[23]

For my last example of the use of a pentagram as a medical symbol I refer to the *Pharmacopoeia Bruxellensis,* published in 1739. The frontispiece of this pharmacopeia, which also appears in the Dutch edition of 1742, shows the interior of a dispensary, in which a chemist and his assistants are working. The back looks out on to a herbal garden. A pentagram with the circumscription SALUS is shown conspicuously above the centre of the arch of the entrance to that garden (Ill. 39).

After the period of Humanism, the old salus sign of the Pythagoreans, the pentagram, which was so much more to this group of philosophers than a mere medical badge or symbol of health, enjoyed something of a renascence. This was due mainly to the study of literary sources and the many discoveries of coins bearing the pentagram,[24] although the latter was endued with a different meaning from that of the Salus Pythagorae. The pentagram, which after the 16th century again became an emblem of health and therefore, by implication, a medical symbol, only faintly echoes the old Pythagorean symbol which, in its new guise, is also somewhat akin to its apotropaic predecessor and was likewise subject to the influence of contemporaneous astrological ideals, so that here and there it did, for all that, become a meaningful medical symbol. Since the 18th century, however, the pentagram has fallen into complete oblivion as a medical

76

Ill. 38. APOTHECARY'S FLAGON AND JARS, GERMANY, 18TH CENTURY.

Ill. 39. PHARMACOPOEIA BRUXELLENSIS, 1739.
FRONTISPIECE BY FRANCOIS HARREWIJN
1700—1764.

78

Ill. 40. JOSJE SMIT, *DUISTERE KRACHTEN* (THE POWERS OF DARKNESS), TAPESTRY (1964) WITH STARFISH (I.E., PENTAGRAM) AS APOTROPAIC CHARM.
IMAGE RISING FROM CARL JUNG'S "COLLECTIVE UNCONSCIOUS".

79

symbol. But it still lives on as an apotropaic talisman, though in most cases completely, or almost completely deprived of all content.

A tapestry by Josje Smit (1964) (Ill. 40) provides a remarkable example of the deliberate use of the pentagram as a charm against the powers of darkness — hence as an apotropaic talisman — despite ignorance of the sign as such. This is the pentagram as an archetype, emerging from what Carl Jung calls the Collective Unconscious.[25]

One can see an intentionally renewed use of the pentagram as a medical symbol in the ex-libris of Dr. J. Fortuyn Droogleever, a woodcut made by Jan Batterman in 1967 [26] (Ill. 41).

Ill. 41. J. FORTUYN DROOGLEEVER'S BOOK-
PLATE. WOODCUT BY JAN BATTER-
MAN, 1967.

NOTES FOR "THE PENTAGRAM AS A MEDICAL SYMBOL"

[1]) Theophrastus Bombastus von Hohenheim, named Paracelsus, Swiss doctor of medicine 1493—1541. He opposed Galenic and Arabian medicine. His alchemistic-mystical speculations considerably influenced later mystics and pietists, including the Moravian Brothers. Goethe's Faust figure was to some extent inspired by Paracelsian ideas.

[2]) Fr. C. Endres, *Die Zahl in Mystik und Glauben der Kulturvölker*, Leipzig 1935, 79-93.

[3]) Heinrich Cornelius Agrippa von Nettesheim, Cologne 1486 - Grenoble 1535. He was an advocate of a return to primitive Christianity. *De occulta Philosophia*, editio princeps, Antwerp, etc. 1531.

[4]) Henricus Cornelius Agrippa ab Nettesheim, *De occulta Philosophia, sive De Magia*, Tomus primus, Liber secundus, cap. XXVII, Lugduni 1724, 193.

[5]) Agrippa ab Nettesheim, *op. cit.*, Tomus secundus, Liber tertius, 75.

[6]) Joannes Pierius Valerianus, *Hieroglyphica sive de sacris* Aegyptiorum, aliarvmque Gentium......, Basle 1567, 351-352, "De Fentalpha", cap. XXXI.

[7]) Valerianus, *op. cit.*, 352 ff.

[8]) Valerianus, ut supra.

[9]) The fact that Valerianus did not consider the pentagram to be a medical symbol is further evidenced by his omission of it form his *Hieroglyphicorum et medicorum emblematum*, Lugduni 1626, 127.

[10]) J. M. Knapp, "Dierenriemmannetje en aderlaatmannetje" (Zodiac Mannikin and Blood-letting Mannikin), *Ciba-Tijdschrift* 9 (1939), 287 ff.

[11]) Vincenzo Cartari, *Le imagini de i dei de gli antichi, . . .*, Venice 1571, 91.

[12]) H. Hofmeier, "Das Pentagram - ein vergessenes Symbol der Medizin", *Materia Medica Nordmark* VIII (1956), 2 ff. (off-print).

[13]) Hollstein mentions a series of 4 plates with Veritas, Justitia, etc., after A. de Weert, 20.2 x 25 cm.
F. W. H. Hollstein, Dutch and Flemish etchings, engravings and woodcuts *c*. 1450—1700, IV, 230, Nos. 167/170.
The engraving to which I am referring is numbered 5, is of the same size and is probably one of the series mentioned by Hollstein.

[14]) Cf. J. Schouten, *The Rod and Serpent of Asklepios, Symbol of Medicine*, Amsterdam-London-New York 1967, 136.

[15]) J. Schouten, *op. cit.*, 143.

82

¹⁶) Cesare Ripa, *Iconologia overo descrittione di diverse imagini cauate dall'* *antichità......*, Roma 1603, 310;
Cesare Ripa, *op. cit.,* 440.

¹⁷) Joh. van Beverwyck, *Wercken der Genees-Konnste, bestaende in den Schat* *der Gesontheyt, Schat der Ongesontheyt, Heelkonste;* Amsterdam 1672: *Schat der Gesontheyt,* 16 ff. (Medical works, consisting of a collection on good health, a collection on ill-health and the art of healing.)

¹⁸) Cf. Ill. 25, p. ......

¹⁹) This work appeared in Geneva as early as 1681.
Johan Conrad Peyer (1653—1712), physician in Schaffhausen, later professor at Heidelberg.
Adriaen Schoonebeek, b. Rotterdam 38th March 1661, d. Moscow 1705; draughtsman, engraver, etcher and publisher. In 1696 librarian to Peter the Great in Moscow.

²⁰) His work was imitated by, *inter alia,* Schoonebeek, by Decker for the *Pharmacopoeia Amstelredamensis* (1701) and Harrewijn for the *Pharma-* *copoeia Bruxellensis* (1702).

²¹) J. Schouten, *The Rod and Serpent of Asklepios, Symbol of Medicine,* Amsterdam-London-New York 1967, 107 ff.

²²) W. F. Daems - L. J. Vandewiele, *Noord- en Zuidnederlandse Stedelijke* *Pharmacopeeën* (Municipal Pharmacopoeias of the Northern and Southern Provinces of the Netherlands), Mortsel-bij-Antwerpen 1955, 116 ff.

²³) Illustrated in Wolfgang-Hagen Hein, *Die Deutsche Apotheke,* Stuttgart 1960, 147.

²⁴) Coin collecting on a considerable scale started in early times and some of these collections provided data for 16th and 17th century numismatic writings.
Cf. Hubert Golzius, *C. Julius Ceasar s. Historiae imperatorum caesarum-* *que Romanorum ex antiquis numismatibus restitutae,* Bruges 1563; idem, *Fasti magistratum et triumphorum Romanorum a.U.c. ad Augusti obitum* *ex antiquis numismatibus,* etc., Bruges 1566; idem, *Caesar Augustus s.* *Historiae imperatorum Caesarumque Romanorum ex antiquis numismatibus* *restitutae,* Bruges 1574; idem, *Sicilia et Magna Graecia s. Historiae urbium* *et populorum Graeciae ex antiquis numismatibus rest.,* Bruges 1576; idem, *Thesaurus rei antiquariae huberrimus ex antiquis tam numismatum quam* *marmorum inscriptionibus* etc., Antwerp 1579; idem, *Graeciae universae* *Asiaeque Minoris et insularum numismata,* Antwerp 1618. (This posthu-mous work is the continuation of *Sicilia et Magna Graecia.)*

²⁵) Cf., J. Schouten, *The Rod and Serpent of Asklepios, Symbol of Medicine,* Amsterdam-London-New York 1967, 223.

²⁶) It was this monograph by J. Schouten, published at The Hague in 1966 under its original Dutch title, *Het Pentagram als medisch teken,* that decided Mr. Fortuyn Droogleever to use the pentagram again as a medical symbol.

SUMMARY

In 1660, the year in which it was founded, the Gouda Surgeons' Guild adopted the pentagram as its emblem. The Gouda Surgeons' Guildhall of 1699 was preserved and now forms part of the "Catharina-Gasthuis" Municipal Museum. Pentagrams are still much in evidence on chairs, cushions, glasswork and the fireplace in this chamber.

Before the Reformation, hence before the abolition of the original guild, Cosmas and Damian were the patron saints of the surgeons at Gouda, as, indeed, almost everywhere else. This could no longer be after the Reformation, so, after careful search for a completely neutral urban constellation, the pentalpha was ultimately adopted as the coat-of-arms of the re-formed guild in 1660.

The pentagram as a medical symbol, like that at Gouda, is to be regarded as a mere remote echo of the Salus Pythagorae, the Pythagorean emblem of health and salvation. The memory of the Pythagorean pentagram as ὑγίεια — hence as a token of health — was kept alive by Humanistic literature, though it did not remain immune to the influence of astrological theories, nor to that of the pentagram as an apotropaic and protective talisman. The latter, which is identical in form to the Pythagorean badge, is far older and was widely used as

85

a magic charm throughout the Middle Ages and in later times; in fact, it still persists here and there, though usually shorn of its inherent implications. As an apotropaic sign, the pentagram was strongly influenced, not only by astrology but by the symbolism of numbers as well.

It is necessary, therefore, to make a clear distinction between the pentagram as an apotropaic charm and the pentagram as a medical symbol, which derives from the Pythagorean symbol. During the 16th century until into the 17th century, the pentagram was also used as a medical emblem and is to be seen in armorial bearings and in the coats-of-arms of guilds, like that of Gouda; likewise in the frontispieces to medical and pharmaceutical works.

In this day and age, the pentagram as a medical symbol has been virtually wiped out of human memory.

BIBLIOGRAPHY

A. Wuttke, *Der deutsche Volksaberglaube,* (1860) 1900[3], 181 ff.

A. Zeising, "Das Pentagramm", *Dt. Vierteljahrsschrift* 31, 1868, 173-226.

S. Seligmann, *Der böse Blick u. Verwandtes,* II, 1910, 293-297.

F. Dornseiff, *Das Alphabet in Mystik und Magie,* Leipzig-Berlin 1922, 84, n. 3.

K. Spiess, *Bauernkunst, ihre Art u. ihr Sinn,* 1925.

W. M. Flinders Petrie, *Decorative Patterns of the Ancient World,* London 1930, pl. 48.

M. Knapp, *Pentagramma Veneris,* 1934.

Allotte de la Fuye, "Le pentagramme pythagoricien sa diffusion, son emploi dans le syllabaire cunéiforme", *Babyloniaca* 14, 1934, 1-36.

F. C. Endres, *Mystik u. Magie der Zahlen,* (1935) 1951[3], 137 ff.

H. Hofmeier, *"Das Pentagram — ein vergessenes Symbol der Medizin".* Materia Medica Nordmark VIII (1956), 2 ff. (offprint).

O. Stöber, *Der Drudenfusz,* 1958[2].

Die Religion in Geschichte und Gegenwart, V, Tübingen 1961, Kol. 209-210.

C. J. de Vogel, *Pythagoras and early Pythagoreanism* (reeks Wijsgerige Teksten en Studies, Universiteit Utrecht), (Phylosophical Discourses and Studies, Utrecht University), Assen 1966.

J. Schouten, *Het pentagram als medisch teken,* Den Haag 1966.

L. Hansmann und Lenz Kriss-Rettenbeck, *Amulett und Talisman,* München 1966.

ILLUSTRATIONS

Ill. 1 Surgeons' Guildhall, 1699.
"Het Catharina-Gasthuis" Municipal Museum of Gouda.

Ill. 2 Tapestried cushion cover with the coat-of-arms of the Gouda Surgeons' Guild 1674.
"Het Catharina-Gasthuis" Municipal Museum of Gouda.

Ill. 3 Device of the Surgeons' Guild of Gouda, 1710.
"Het Catharina-Gasthuis" Municipal Museum of Gouda.

Ill. 4 Glass goblet belonging to the Surgeons' Guild of Gouda, showing coat-of-arms with Cosmas and Damian on either side.
"Het Catharina-Gasthuis" Municipal Museum of Gouda.

Ill. 5 Testimonial issued by Cornelis Bleuland, surgeon in Gouda, in favour of Adrianus v. Bergen, 1st September 1785.
Gouda Municipal Records Office.

Ill. 6 The pentagram on a frieze in the synagogue of Capernaum, 3rd century A.D.

Ill. 7   Pentagrams on Jewish jars, probably 5th century B.C.

Ill. 8   Inscription on a tombstone in Tortosa, Spain, 4th century A.D.

Ill. 9   Amphora with the pentagram depicted escutcheon. Munich.

Ill. 10   Stater of Melos with pentagram.

Ill. 11   Stone relief with pentagram, 10th/11th century. In the 13th century this fragment and others were used to line a front. Split, Jugoslavia.

Ill. 12   Woodcut from *Pluemen der Tugent,* Augsburg 1486. The pentagram on the threshold prevents a witch from entering the byre.

Ill. 13   Israhel van Meckenen, *c.* 1445-1503, Nativitas. The hexagram on the cradle is identical here to the pentagram.

Ill. 14   Pentagram (Drudenfusz) on the inner side of the head of the cradle. Two angels are depicted holding Christ's monogram, IHS, on the outer side of the foot, 1579.
          Bayerisches Nationalmuseum, Munich.

Ill. 15   Votive tablet from Stadeleck, 1675. There is a protective pentagram on the outer side of the foot of the bedstead.
          Bayerisches Nationalmuseum, Kriss collection, Munich.

Ill. 16   House-sign with pentagram on a façade at Groenlo.

Ill. 17   Seal of Jan Willem Lakenmansz., 1331.
          Municipal Records, Gouda.

90

Ill. 30   Athanasius Kircher, *Ars Magnetica,* Roma 1654, frontispiece (detail).

Ill. 31   Hygieia with hexagram (for pentagram), illustration in *Schat der Gesondtheyt* by Joh. van Beverwyck, Amsterdam 1672.

Ill. 32   Joh. Nicolaus Pechlin, *De Purgantibus Exercitatio,* Leyden and Amsterdam 1672.

Ill. 33   *Jani Leoniceci Veronensis* (Joh. Nicolaus Pechlin) *Metamorphosis aesculapii et Apollinis Pancreatici,* 1673.

Ill. 34   Gerardus Blasius, *Ontleeding des menschelijken lichaems* (Anatomy of the human body), Amsterdam 1675, frontispiece.

Ill. 35   Johan Conrad Peyer, *Parerga anatomica,* Amsterdam 1682. Frontispiece by Adriaen Schoonebeek.

Ill. 36   Johan Conrad Peyer, *Parergo Anatomica et Medica,* Amsterdam 1682. Title-page, woodcut.

Ill. 37   *Pharmacopoea Harlemensis,* 1693. Frontispiece by Romein de Hooghe.

Ill. 38   Apothecary's flagon and jars, Germany, 18th century.

Ill. 39   Pharmacopoeia Bruxellensis, 1739. Frontispiece by François Harrewijn 1700-1764.

Ill. 40   Josje Smit, *Duistere Krachten* (the powers of darkness), tapestry (1964) with starfish (i.e., pentagram as apotropaic charm.
Image rising from Carl Jung's "Collective Unconscious".

Ill. 41   J. Fortuyn Droogleever's book-plate. Woodcut by Jan Batterman, 1967.

INDEX

Simple figures stand for page numbers; these followed by a hyphenated
'n.' and number show the appropriate note.

93

95